ACTION SPORTS

# KARTING

**Joe Herran and Ron Thomas**

CHELSEA HOUSE
PUBLISHERS
A Haights Cross Communications ✦ Company
Philadelphia

This edition first published in 2004 in the United States of America by Chelsea House Publishers, a subsidiary of Haights Cross Communications.

Chelsea House Publishers
1974 Sproul Road, Suite 400
Broomall, PA 19008-0914

The Chelsea House world wide web address is www.chelseahouse.com

Library of Congress Cataloging-in-Publication Data

Herran, Joe.
    Karting / Joe Herran and Ron Thomas.
    p. cm. — (Action sports)

    Includes index.
    Contents: What is karting? — Karting gear — Driver's gear — Karting safely — Maintaining the kart — The karting circuit — Skills and techniques — In competition — Formula Super A: World Championship kart racing — Other kart-racing competitions — Karting champions — Then and now — Related action sports.

    ISBN 0-7910-7535-4
    1. Karting—Juvenile literature. [1. Karting.] I. Thomas, Ron. II. Title. III. Series: Action sports (Chelsea House Publishers).
    GV1029.5.H47 2004
    796.7'6—dc21

2003001181

First published in 2003 by
MACMILLAN EDUCATION AUSTRALIA PTY LTD
627 Chapel Street, South Yarra, Australia, 3141

Associated companies and representatives throughout the world.

Edited by Renée Otmar, Otmar Miller Consultancy Pty Ltd, Melbourne
Text and cover design by Karen Young
Illustrations by Nives Porcellato and Andy Craig
Page layout by Raul Diche
Photo research by Legend Images

Printed in China

**Acknowledgements**
The author and the publisher are grateful to the following for permission to reproduce copyright materials:

Cover photograph: karts in grid position for the start of a race, courtesy of Vitantonio Liuzzi/ www.liuzzi.com

Australian Picture Library/Corbis, p. 30 (top); Daimler Chrysler AG, p. 29; Mike Ashton, Drag Racing Photography/www.dragpixs.co.nz, p. 30 (bottom); Ferrari Press Office, p. 4; Getty Images, p. 28 (left); KartOz, p. 25 (bottom); Bill Kistler at www.racepixs.com, p. 27 (left); Vitantonio Liuzzi/www.liuzzi.com, pp. 11, 12, 18–19, 22–23, 24, 26 (left); Amber Martinez-Engstrom, p. 27 (right); Red Bolt, pp. 5 (top), 7, 9, 16, 17, 20; Sutton Motorsport Images, p. 25 (top); Toyota Motorsport, p. 26 (right); Michael Wintrip, pp. 5 (bottom), 10; www.corporatekarting.com/kartinghistory.htm, p. 28 (right).

While every care has been taken to trace and acknowledge copyright, the publisher tenders their apologies for any accidental infringement where copyright has proved untraceable. Where the attempt has been unsuccessful, the publisher welcomes information that would redress the situation.

# CONTENTS

# INTRODUCTION

In this book you will read about:
* karts and the kart driver's gear
* safety measures used to keep kart drivers safe
* kart-driving skills and techniques
* karting **circuits** and competitions
* some of the top karting drivers in competition today
* the history of karting since the 1950s.

## In the beginning

The first go-carts were built to run downhill. They were built without engines. These go-carts were used in competitions, such as the American Soap Box Derby, which is still held in the United States. The motorized go-cart was invented in 1956 by U.S. racing car mechanic Art Ingels and his friend, Lou Borelli. Based in California, these inventors built a simple steel-tubing frame and fixed four wheels to it—one to each corner. The engine, which was similar to those used in lawnmowers, was mounted behind the driver's seat. Go-cart racing soon became very popular as a sport, and go-carting became known as karting.

Formula One World Champion Michael Schumacher briefly returned to karting in 2001.

## Karting today

From simple beginnings karting has spread to countries around the world to become a highly organized, professional, international motor sport. Many of the world's top Formula One drivers started their driving careers as karting drivers.

 **Warning** This is not a how-to book for aspiring karters. It is intended as an introduction to the exciting world of karting, and a look at where the sport has come from and where it is heading.

# WHAT IS KARTING?

Karting is an inexpensive way for people to enjoy the thrill and excitement of motor racing. It is a motor-racing sport open to people of all ages. Some of the youngest drivers are just 8 years old, and there is no upper age limit!

Karting is a fun weekend activity for families. At specially built indoor and outdoor kart circuits, young drivers can learn to drive in a safe and supervised environment.

Karting is also a serious motor-racing competition with race meetings held at local club, national and international levels. In 2001, the Commission Internationale de Karting (CIK), a member of the Fédération Internationale de l'Automobile (FIA), which governs Formula One motor sports, established a new World Championship for karting. World Championship karting races by professional drivers are now held in countries around the world. The CIK–FIA has established a sporting code of rules and regulations for World Championship karting, as well as technical rules to ensure that karts are safe.

↗ Karting is a great family sport.

↗ Karting races are held in countries around the world on specially built karting circuits.

5

# KARTING GEAR

## The kart

The kart is a specially designed and tested machine. Karts come in different classifications from the least powerful 60 **cc** for 8- to 12-year-olds, to 250 cc superkarts used in international competitions.

The main parts of a kart are the frame, or chassis, engine, tires and brakes.

### Frame

The frame, or chassis, is made of pieces of steel tubing. The tubing pieces are welded together in a way that allows the chassis to absorb the shock of bumps. It is low to the ground, and the driver's seat is just about an inch (2 to 3 centimeters) above the track. Wheels are attached to the corners of the chassis, and brakes are built into the frame.

Disc brakes

Accelerator and brake pedals

Exhaust pipe

Front bumper

Rear bumper

Steering wheel

Seat

Axle

Chain

Fuel tank

Engine

Frame or chassis

Wheels and tires

**PARTS OF THE KART**

## Engine

Most engines designed and built for kart racing are two-cycle engines. The fuel used is a mixture of oil and gasoline. It is burned inside the engine to produce the energy needed to run the kart at speeds of between 53 and 93 miles (85 and 150 kilometers) per hour, depending on the size of the engine. In recent times, four-cycle engines have been built and fitted to karts.

## Brakes

Brakes are used to slow the kart so that the driver can make turns safely, and to stop the kart in an emergency or at the end of a driving session. Disc brakes are preferred, because water can accumulate in drum brakes, causing them to fail. Disc brakes fling off any water, so they are more reliable.

## Tires

Specially designed rubber tires for karts are light and simply constructed. They provide good grip during a race. Tires at the front of the kart are smaller in diameter than the tires at the rear. Two types of kart tires are available: **slick** tires for use when the circuit is dry, and patterned, or grooved, tires for use in wet weather.

**A TWO-CYCLE ENGINE**

## ACTION FACT

CIK–FIA has ruled that by 2005 all karts competing in World Championship races must be fitted with four-cycle engines. Although four-cycle engines are heavier, they do not pollute the air as much as two-cycle engines do.

# DRIVER'S
# GEAR

## Helmet and visor

All karting drivers must wear a helmet to protect their head during a fall. Helmets for child drivers are made of lightweight fiberglass, while adult drivers wear heavier helmets with a **Kevlar** shell. Helmets have adjustable chinstraps and a ventilation system to keep the driver's head cool. A visor is fitted to the helmet. The visor has several see-through strips on it, and when the top strip becomes dirty, the driver simply peels it off.

## Driving suit

Karters wear a one-piece suit made of **nylon** fabric lined with soft cotton. Special panels in the shoulders and underarms help with ventilation to keep the driver comfortable.

## Driving vest

The driving vest is a padded garment worn under the suit on the upper body to protect the ribs and torso from bruising on rough surfaces. The vest is made of a cotton-covered foam.

## Neck brace

The neck brace is a cotton-covered block of foam that supports the helmet and protects the driver from neck strain. Neck braces are highly recommended for young drivers.

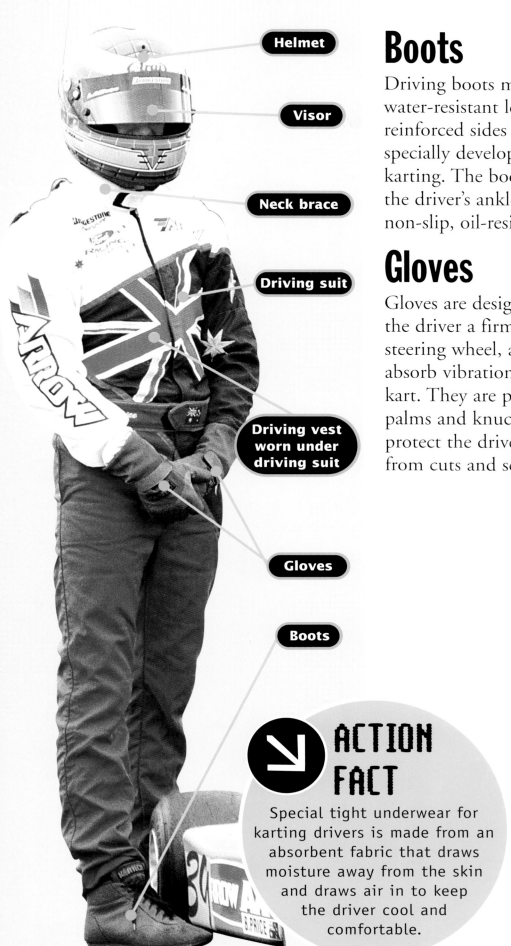

Helmet

Visor

Neck brace

Driving suit

Driving vest worn under driving suit

Gloves

Boots

# Boots

Driving boots made of water-resistant leather with reinforced sides have been specially developed for karting. The boots protect the driver's ankles and have non-slip, oil-resistant soles.

# Gloves

Gloves are designed to give the driver a firm grip on the steering wheel, and to help absorb vibrations from the kart. They are padded on the palms and knuckles to protect the driver's hands from cuts and scratches.

## ACTION FACT

Special tight underwear for karting drivers is made from an absorbent fabric that draws moisture away from the skin and draws air in to keep the driver cool and comfortable.

# KARTING
# SAFELY

Karting is one of the safest forms of motor racing. Karts are built low to the ground and are difficult to turn over. Drivers are required to wear specially designed and approved driving suits, gloves, boots and helmets for personal safety.

## Obeying the rules

Karting drivers should follow these basic rules to keep themselves and others safe and injury-free:

- check that the helmet is clean and undamaged
- check that the visor is cleaned after every race
- check that gloves, the driving suit and other protective clothes are clean and in good condition
- know the basic skills of speed control, turning and braking
- know how to slow down if losing control of the kart
- look ahead for obstacles and signs of danger
- obey the rules made to protect drivers and spectators
- have had a practice run on a new course
- never drive alone when practicing, in case of an accident
- drink plenty of water to avoid **dehydration**, muscle cramps and loss of concentration.

Drivers wear protective clothing and safety barriers are placed around the circuit to keep drivers safe.

# Getting ready to drive and driver fitness

All karting drivers, especially those drivers competing at national and international levels of the sport, need to be physically fit. Strong, fit muscles are needed by drivers, who must squeeze their bodies into the cramped space of a kart. Neck and back muscles need to be strong to cope with the forces placed on them during a race. Drivers must learn how to deal with crashes and accidents by learning to relax the body. Relaxing the body reduces the likelihood of broken bones in an accident.

Drivers keep fit by jogging, cycling, swimming or working out in a gymnasium. These activities improve driver reflexes, concentration and balance. A good diet also keeps a driver fit and race ready.

## Stretching before driving

Because the driver is so close to the ground when sitting in the kart, some exercises and stretches before racing will prepare the body for the event.

◤ Karting champion Vitantonio Liuzzi keeps fit by cycling and lifting weights.

# MAINTAINING THE
# KART

A good driver always looks after his kart to ensure the best performance. Regular kart maintenance includes:

- cleaning and drying the kart after all races; parts of the kart left wet may rust
- washing the air filter with warm, soapy water
- inspecting tires for damage and wear
- checking tire pressure
- checking that the brakes are working properly
- checking that the chain is well lubricated with oil
- checking that fuel is at proper levels
- checking to make sure that there are no loose or missing screws or bolts anywhere on the kart
- checking the chassis joints for cracks
- straightening any parts of the kart that are bent
- checking the wheel alignment to ensure that the weight on each wheel is equal.

Drivers and mechanics can check their karts in **pit** areas beside the track.

# THE KARTING CIRCUIT

There are hundreds of karting circuits in countries around the world. Each has its own special design, with a straight section and left and right turns. In 2001, CIK–FIA set out some rules for the design and construction of safe karting circuits. These include:

- a circuit must be 1 to 1.6 miles (1.7 to 2.5 kilometers) in length and 26.2 to 42.7 feet (8 to 13 meters) wide
- the surface of the circuit should be **asphalt**
- the starting area must provide space for 36 karts
- there must be a pit area (fenced park) beside the track for drivers and their teams
- there must be a fire-fighting service, with several fire extinguishers available at the circuit
- the track must be bordered on all sides by open areas, 3 feet (1 meter) wide and have safety barriers
- all spectator areas must be enclosed with fences at least 4 feet (1.2 meters) high
- there must be at least 87.5 yards (80 meters) between the start and the first corner of a circuit.

Karting circuits are designed to keep drivers and spectators safe.

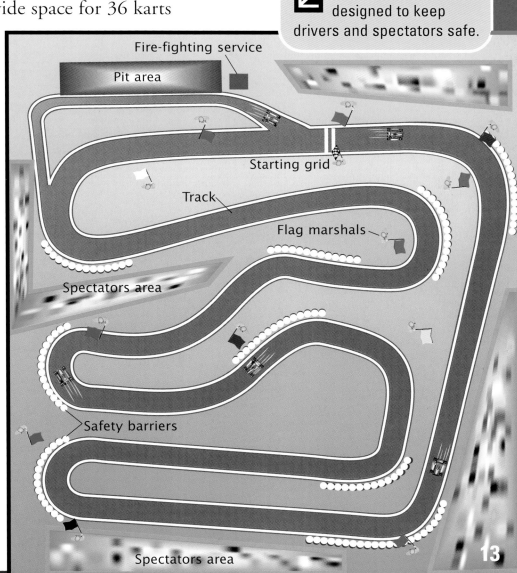

Fire-fighting service

Pit area

Starting grid

Track

Flag marshals

Spectators area

Safety barriers

Spectators area

13

# SKILLS AND
# TECHNIQUES

## Basic driving skills

A kart driver aims to complete a lap of the circuit in the fastest time possible. To do this, the driver must have learned the three basic skills of kart driving:

- braking
- accelerating
- turning.

### Braking

Brakes are used to slow the kart during turns, in emergencies and to stop the kart at the end of a driving session. Skilled drivers know when and how to apply brakes safely. For example, the brake is used to slow the kart as it approaches a turn and before the turn is started. As a general rule it is best not to brake after turning the steering wheel as this may send the kart into a spin. Brakes are best applied with the wheels straight.

### Accelerating

When a driver puts pressure on the accelerator pedal, fuel is delivered to the engine, which drives the kart forward. A driver learns when to **accelerate** and when to slow down. For example, a driver knows to slow down when approaching a turn, but on entering the turn accelerates to complete the turn and return to the **straight** at top speed.

- - - - Driving line

Braking

Accelerating

## Turning

A driver learns always to take the shortest course around a corner and at the fastest, safest speed. Most turns are made from the outside of the course to reduce the angle of the turn. The turn should be smooth, and the driver should not make any sudden movements to the steering wheel.

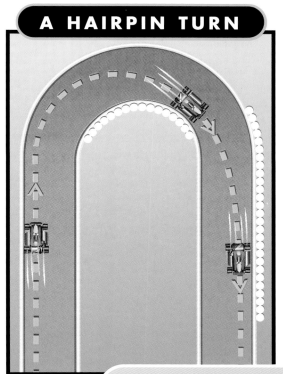

The driving lines to be followed by a skilled driver at corners of different angles.

# Steering straight and looking ahead

When driving on straight sections of the circuit, it is important to keep the wheels straight to maintain maximum speed. A driver also looks ahead when driving. Looking over the shoulder leads to loss of concentration on the road ahead.

# Passing an opponent

The best and safest place for one driver to pass another is on the straight. The driver wishing to pass must accelerate to speed by the other kart. However, most passing is done at corners. The driver wanting to pass follows a different line to the driver in front, and tries to pass on the inside during the turn.

# IN COMPETITION

## Kart racing

All drivers wanting to compete in kart racing must have a **karting license** and be a member of a karting club. There are karting races for various age groups. The youngest is for 8- to 12-year-olds who drive 60 cc karts in the Cadet or Midget class. Junior class races are open to licensed kart drivers aged 13 to 16. Senior classes are for drivers 16 years and older. Professional class drivers compete in the Formula Super A World Championship.

These young drivers are competing in a Midget class competition.

# Setting up

The driver makes adjustments to the kart to ensure that it performs at its best, taking into account weather conditions and track surface. Most kart race drivers have a team to help with the preparation of the kart for racing. Younger drivers may have parents or other adults working as a team to help prepare the kart for racing, while professional drivers usually have a crew of mechanics to make sure the kart is ready. The set-up includes making adjustments to the chassis and to such things as tire pressure, wheel spacing and seat position.

# Checking for safety

Before races begin, officials called scrutineers check that all karts entered in a race are safe. The scrutineers check that the kart is in good working order, and also check that drivers are wearing proper protective clothing. Other officials, called marshals, check safety barriers around the track and make sure that the track is free from dangerous materials. Flag marshals are posted on the bends to signal to the drivers if there is any danger.

↗ Before a race, all karts are given a safety check.

# Practicing on the track

Before the qualifying round all drivers are given the opportunity to take a practice drive on the track. Practice enables the drivers to learn the layout of the track and experience the turns and straights, so that the driver and their team can plan a driving **strategy** for the race. The driver is also able to test the kart to make sure it is properly set up for the race. Practice also gives each driver a chance to study their competitors, noting their strategies for driving the course.

# Briefing the drivers

Before the races begin, a meeting of all competitors is organized by the race director. The drivers are reminded of the rules and regulations for the event, and about the safety procedures for the course. Drivers have a chance at the briefing meeting to ask questions about the race, the circuit and the rules.

# Qualifying heats

Qualifying heats, or races, are run before the main race. The fastest drivers earn a spot in the final race. A kart's position on the starting **grid** for the final race is determined by how well they do in the qualifying heats. The driver who has the fastest time in the qualifying heats will be awarded **pole position**. The pole-position driver has the choice of first position on either the left or right side of the starting grid.

↗ Drivers line up on the grid for the start of a race.

# Positioning on the grid

The grid determines how the karts line up for the start of the race. There are two rows of karts on the grid. Before the race begins, the drivers make a warm-up lap of the circuit, keeping their grid positions. This warm-up lap allows the engines, tires and brakes to warm up. As soon as the karts return to the grid, the starter signals the beginning of the race by turning the red starting lights off.

# Some of the rules of competition

These are some of the rules which apply at kart-racing tracks.

- Drivers are responsible for the safe condition and operation of their own karts.
- All competitors must maintain a neat appearance.
- All fuels and other **flammable** liquids must be stored in metal containers.
- Alcohol and illegal drugs are prohibited.
- All karts must have a chain guard over the chain so drivers do not injure themselves on it.
- Exhaust systems must be set up so fumes are carried away from the driver.
- A driver who has to stop during the race must make sure that the kart will not cause any danger or be hazardous to other drivers.
- A driver entering the track from the pits must do so in a manner that will cause no danger to other karts.
- Any kart leaking fuel during an event must leave the track immediately.

# Hand signals

Drivers use hand signals to communicate with each other during races.

- When a driver is going into the pits or coming back onto the track, it is compulsory for the driver to raise a hand as a signal to other drivers.
- If a driver has to stop on or beside the track, the driver must raise a hand to signal passing drivers.
- During a race, a driver who is given a flag signal by a marshal must raise a hand to show the marshal that the flag signal has been understood.

↗ Drivers use hand signals to communicate with each other during races.

# Flags for safety

In order to keep kart racing as safe as possible, drivers are kept informed about what is happening during a race by marshals who use flags to signal drivers about conditions on the track. Each flag has a different meaning.

- A green flag indicates that the track is clear for racing.

- A red flag tells drivers to stop because the track is hazardous and unsafe for racing.

- A yellow flag warns drivers to slow down, use caution and prepare to stop. The track may be blocked by an accident, people, an animal or an object from another kart. No passing is allowed when the yellow flag is displayed.

- A blue flag indicates that a faster competitor is trying to overtake and the slower driver must move out of the way as safely as possible.

- A white flag indicates the final lap of the race.

- A black flag warns a driver that the marshals have noticed that the driver is doing something that may lead to **disqualification**. A black flag with the kart number tells a driver to reduce speed and stop at the pit. A mechanical defect has been noticed.

- The checkered flag indicates that the race is over.

# FORMULA SUPER A: WORLD CHAMPIONSHIP
# KART RACING

In 2001, the CIK, a member of the FIA, established a new World Championship for karting. This competition is based on Formula One Grand Prix racing, and has kart-racing events in countries around the world.

## The formula

The formula, or technical rules or regulations, for karts used in Formula Super A are that:

- karts must be fitted with a 100 cc engine without a gearbox
- karts must have front and rear bumpers not more than 7.9 inches (20 centimeters) from the ground
- racing numbers must appear on the side box panels of the kart, and the driver's name must appear on the front facing panel
- the driver's seat must be designed to prevent the driver from moving toward the sides or front when cornering or braking
- brake and accelerator pedals must not protrude forward of the chassis or the bumper
- the fuel tank must be securely fixed to the chassis and have a capacity of at least 2 gallons (8 liters)
- the kart's tires must be no more than 4.9 inches (12.5 centimeters) in diameter.

# The team

Formula Super A karts are constructed and maintained by mechanics, engineers and drivers known as the team. Engine and tire manufacturers' names and logos and the names and logos of sponsors appear on the kart. The teams of the first 15 finishers in a race are awarded points. At the end of the season, the title of World Champion Team is awarded to the team that has scored the greatest number of points.

The names and logos of sponsors are painted on the kart and appear on the driver's clothing.

# The event

The Formula Super A Championship series consists of five events held throughout the year. At each event there are free practice drives, qualifying heats in which the drivers are timed and finals races. All qualifying drivers, those with the fastest times in the heats, race in the two finals races, called Race 1 and Race 2. Finals races cover a distance of 15.4 miles (25 kilometers). Points are awarded to the first 15 finishers in each race. The points range from 25 for the winner to one point for the driver in 15th place. At the end of the series of five events, the driver with the most points is declared the World Champion Driver.

**ACTION FACT**

All karts must meet CIK–FIA specifications and must be inspected by officials before they are allowed to race.

# The podium ceremony

The drivers who finish the race in first, second and third positions attend a prize-giving ceremony on the **podium** after the race. Standing on the podium, the drivers receive their prizes while the national anthem of the winner's country is played.

Drivers are awarded prizes at the end of the first round of the Formula Super A Championship in 2001.

# OTHER KART-RACING
# COMPETITIONS

## Enduro

**Enduro** is kart racing held on large asphalt road courses, such as the Daytona International Speedway in the United States. The races in this class of kart racing can last from 20 to 45 minutes. Drivers reach speeds of up to 93 miles (150 kilometers) per hour in karts with 100 cc engines, and up to 149 miles (240 kilometers) per hour in superkarts with 250 cc engines. Due to the high speeds reached in competition, enduro is an event for experienced kart drivers. **Aerodynamic** design is an important feature of enduro karts. It enables drivers to reach very high speeds.

↗ Enduro karts have an aerodynamic design and are raced on road courses.

## Dirt

Dirt karting is a popular form of kart racing. Children from 7 years of age can compete. Races are conducted using sprint kart chassis set up for making turns on oval dirt and clay speedways. Some dirt karting tracks are indoors.

↗ This driver is competing in a dirt championship for 7- to 10-year-olds.

# KARTING
# CHAMPIONS

The sport of karting had simple beginnings and was seen as a child's sport. Over the past 20 years, however, karting has become increasingly popular and has attracted professional drivers. Top drivers in the Formula Super A (FSA) competition come from European countries and from the United States. Competitions of all standards are held on tracks around the world, from the local track for amateurs to the World Champion FSA competitions.

## ↗ Vitantonio Liuzzi

- Born August 6, 1981, Italy
- Began in the Italian karting Cadet class at age 10
- Competed in the final round of the Karting World Championship in Germany in 2001, competing against Michael Schumacher, the Champion Formula One driver and former karting driver

### Career highlights

- Won second place in the Italian Karting Championships in 1994 and 1995
- Joined Formula Super A category, won the Brazilian Karting Prix in São Paulo, came seventh in the World Karting Championships in 1997
- Won the European Karting Championships in 1999
- Came second in the World Cup, in Montegi, in 2000
- CIK–FIA Karting World Champion in 2001
- Joined German Opal Formula 3 racing team as lead driver in 2002

## ↗ Ryan Briscoe

- Born September 24, 1981, Australia
- Started karting in Australia at age 12
- Moved to Italy in 1997 and started competing in the European karting competition

### Career highlights

- Won the Australian Junior Yamaha Kart Championships in 1994
- Competed in the World Kart Championship race in Portugal in 1995
- Began racing karts in Europe for CRG, an Italian kart maker, in 1997
- Won the United States Kart Championships in 1998
- Won the Italian Open Kart Championship in 1999
- Won the Italian Formula Renault Championship in 2001
- Won the International Formula 3000 Championship in 2002

# ↗ Phil Carlson

- Born June 6, 1979, Gallup, New Mexico
- Started racing with the San Diego Karting Association in the Junior Sportsman class
- Has competed in the Southwest Series of the International Karting Federation championships in the United States
- Overall goal is to drive in Formula One events with Michael Schumacher, his favorite driver

## Career highlights

- Champion San Diego Karting Association, Junior Sportsman class, in 1995
- National Champion, International Karting Federation, Sportsman class, in 1996
- Champion Southwest Super series in 1998
- National Champion, International Karting Federation Formula A, in 1999
- Winner Horstman Invitation, Champion Southwest Super series, 2nd International Karting Federation, in 2000
- Top Rookie SKUSA ProMoto Tour in 2001

# ↗ Amber Martinez-Engstrom

- Born July 31, 1986, Saginaw, Texas
- Has been racing in United States karting competitions for four years
- Her 6-year-old sister, Kaley, is also a karting driver

## Career highlights

- Won third place in the North Texas Kartways (NTK) summer series in 1998
- Kart National Champion in 2000
- Won the Kart Southern Regional Series, Kartways of Arkansas in 2001
- Won the NTK Spring 5 of the Spring series in 2001
- Came sixth in the Kart Nationals and fourth in the Kart Southern Regional Series in 2001

| 1956 | Late 1950s | 1959 | 1960 | 1960s | 1964 |
|------|-----------|------|------|-------|------|
| The go-cart was invented in California by racing car mechanic Art Ingels and his friend, Lou Borelli. They built a simple chassis, using a steel tube framework, four wheels and a 100 cc lawnmower engine. | The first kart track was built in Azusa, California. | The first world karting title was won by American Jim Yamane. | Karting circuits were built in Britain, mainly at unused airfields. | The Commission Internationale de Karting (CIK) was formed in Paris, France. The first karting magazines appeared in the United States. | The first CIK-organized world championship event for 100 cc karts was won by Guido Sala of Italy. |

1950s

1960s

| 1966 | 1970s | 1980s | 1981 | 1983 | 2001 |
|---|---|---|---|---|---|
| Susanna Raganelli became the first woman to win the Karting World Championships. | Kart designers mounted the engines on the side of the vehicle rather than at the rear. | National karting organizations formed throughout the world. These organizations recognized different forms of karting and developed formal rules for them. | The World Championship formula was changed from 100 cc to 135 cc. | Another world championship class was introduced, the Formula E for 250 cc geared karts. | The CIK–FIA established a new World Championship for Karting, using Formula Super A Karts. The first electric karts were designed and built. |

2001

29

# RELATED ACTION
# SPORTS

## Soap Box Derby

The Soap Box Derby is a vehicle racing event for young people from around the United States and the world. It has been run in the United States since 1934. World Championship finals are held each August at Derby Downs, in Akron, Ohio. The young competitors build their own carts, which do not have engines, and race them downhill. Boys and girls aged from 9 to 16 compete.

## Junior Drag Racing

The National Hot Rod Association (NHRA) Junior Drag Racing League began in the United States in 1992. It gives boys and girls aged from 8 to 17 the opportunity to race in half-scale **dragsters**, which are powered by five-horsepower engines, at speeds of up to 87 miles (140 kilometers) per hour.

Competing drivers race on approximately 130 tracks built across the United States, Canada and Puerto Rico. Competing drivers, who must be licensed to drive and be members of a drag-racing club, wear helmets and other protective clothing when racing.

↗ The goals of the Soap Box Derby program are to teach young people the basic skills of building carts, the spirit of competition and commitment to continue a project once it has begun.

↘ Qualified drag-racing drivers compete each year for prizes which include college scholarships.

# GLOSSARY

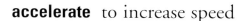

**accelerate** to increase speed

**aerodynamic** qualities of the kart that affect the way it moves through the air, particularly what makes it travel faster

**asphalt** a black sticky substance made of oil and bitumen

**cc** cubic capacity, relating to the size of the engine

**circuits** racetracks

**dehydration** the loss of water or moisture from the body

**disqualification** when a competitor is taken out of a race because they have broken the rules

**dragsters** cars designed for drag racing

**enduro** a type of karting endurance race

**flammable** easily set on fire

**Formula One** racing specially designed cars on purpose-built circuits

**grid** area on the track where the karts line up for the start of the race

**karting license** permission to drive a kart, having learned the basics of karting

**Kevlar** a material that is extremely strong and heat-resistant

**nylon** a synthetic fabric that is very strong and elastic

**pit** an area near the track where teams and drivers work on karts

**podium** the place where drivers receive their awards after the race

**pole position** the first position in the starting grid, slightly ahead of the others

**slick** refers to tires that are smooth and have little or no tread

**straight** the part of a race circuit without curves

**strategy** planning how a race will be run

# INDEX